the parts of the body that stink

SJ Fowler

This softcover edition was published in 2024

Hesterglock Press
The Blue Room
25 Wathen Road
Bristol
BS6 5BY UK

hesterglock.net

all content ©SJ Fowler 2024
cover design: Babak Safari
layout: SJ Fowler & Bob Modem

ISBN: 978-1739556600

contents

nose

The whole of sexuality and not merely anal eroticism
is threatened with falling victim to the organic
repression consequent upon man's adoption of the
erect posture and the lowering in value of the sense
of smell.

Sigmund Freud

to be good
one. homo sapien:
creature that smells
least and stinks most

creature that
when you smell you smell
your own
nose first

for the front of the mind
smell then shifting
size of sensation
found through your nose
you sniff yourself and ask

what is that smell?

the smell of living
you think
and know
nothing

a gap

that smell that follows you into all beds

all you've ever been in

for birth
you don't remember

to what you won't see coming

the smell of something you are passing

the strange smell
that external orientates
and everyone
around you is

but where has that in sight taken you?

it has squeezed out your pores
a yellow small snail liquid
and how do you pinch?
fingers, to the nose,
that you put on teeth
that you don't wipe and get into trousers
that you move around well
like rank

condensed around you into the scent
of something animal
you squint at the scents around and see

by not washing yourself nonstop you understand
the soup of your body is a lack of suspicion

you have out loud
you wear traces of wee like cologne
your perfume to pull what moves from the nose, to the mind

and this is you as smell
telling you of how
much your foot stank
to rub your sweaty hands on your dry feet
and wipe it under your own nose
again and again
as a happy releif

how much your pits stink is sky writing
of a bad bird with a foggy tail

how much your sexual organs leak smell beyond
your clever clever better better is not sad, joe john julie jemima

how little you win arguments with your nose

how often your fingers nearly frostbitten won't fall off

you wish so

so you could pick them again

and place them on heaters

to watch them tap back to life

and over by the wall

about the scent of unreadable

lectures you listen from the lonely

unreliable

collected consciousness of thinking

lessons given by those

who never smelt of nothing

until they died

of this the smell

of you scratching

the smell of sex you've left yourself no space to appreciate

the smell of the sound of the summer

the smell of the horn

the smell of amazon prime

the smell of the hunt being hunted up the nose

your farm-life too

knock your angry

not smell, travail

travel

smells of sinkhole

foreign legions of women and men together
of clothes changing

of toilet trips
during periods of illness.

this is smells of being
picked up

and stashed

this the smell of your stupid drugs why
this the cheap supermarket and their technical fragrance

this is the change in you
the cheese without milk
the bodywater feature tepid
the slowing fountain of leak

this is those you meet who have no access to showers

the smell changes taste, but doesn't affect sight? You ask

Soap. You think

Nothing is odourless. You think.

a small pool of blood
gets bigger behind your back
you can't smell for the blood is not
leaking from your nose
you can't reach to raise it to you, on your fingers
you walk around smelling like the iron that is in it
you didn't know
you thought you smelled of that the
smells like your dad disappointed
smells like now you see animals are watching to see if you fall
over smells like if you were in the sea, forget about it
even the seals would eat you

you never thought humans are tragic because
they can never be as sure of others as animals
as you are of ourself

you recall o my friends there is no friend, said aristotle

and you think what is the smell of regrowth? of a limb

humans are sharks with faces
and smell so
and walk over
and look back at you
and it the noseless face you see in your memory that teaches
you nothing but
get ready

you stop as people in the street stop
you and say you've got blood on your back
after the first person has said it you start to reply yeah yeah
I know
I was bleeding before you even heard that saw that smelled that
that blood of steam
and what does iron smell like to someone
who has never held anything iron?
doesn't know metal
new. new smell.

the metallic smell of comfort

of dishwashers washing your bastard clothes

of your fingers and their clawing reach slippery with another's

blood

for someone who is congested

even constipated coagulateda

you do you without doing anything about you

you'll take care of you later

you don't even say thank you

to these strangers

who warn you

and cover their noses

you think, can you imagine what nurses like that have to

smell? but this is a passing thought and you start to heal

you are a human being with hands

alive of a kind in fingers

with painted nails

where you've known no alternative

no choice on

the trimethylaminuria

or ulcerative colitis

awful cause of our own extreme odour
that won't be treated

perhaps the condition is undiagnosable?
perhaps new?
perhaps being in question never goes to doctor?

the latter is silly, for you definitely go the doctor all the time
even if you've got a minor problem

For you are you who
chooses their own adventure

the face of people in olfactory
Revelation creates for you an
existence for you you didn't
have before and that's before
and that's not good you lose

loved ones of a clean kind and maybe friends, jobs,
yet you can't explain.
what may be bodily, but is the wrong sort of self

love for others noses
but it is and it's growing
the love of your own rinse

of fish, of the initials B and O
of cheese and presence
of what you are in the fourth sense

the smell smelling
you start smelling, mean

the way of sense, a newfound place, is through the internal
emanation

these wounds
as far removed from the smells that make the animal's share
of life
are there

the human being that is you smells them
and shares them with the few remaining
those with dull senses alive

you speak of a body as if it was all you are
because you now believe this

unescaping the way others can
with flush
you live to breed bacteria
once a day, for food and air
to find at last
the smell
that really is you

what is funny
on the nose
is beyond waits new
around one understanding

what is the smell of the trap?

how old are you, someone asks?
you look around, see no mouths at all
you sniff the air

when you are hot, you're bothered
you sigh endless sighs

your hands curl into a ball like a monkeys paw
to think of how monkey's smell
the great apes and their reeking fur
all over the jungle

children don't like you
and you don't know them
it's lovely to talk to other people's cats
cats who smell very little but you don't be fooled
they know when you're around inside their little pink triangle
noses
and they tell
they tell others and they come
and you hide
and you run
and then you get worse even
and then you cry
and that is why
the cats smell the blood on your back
dried and flaking

and that is the only reason they like you

they smell the smell of your unwashed fingers on the way back
from where
you are coming from

luckily you
the permanently odorous
there is the internet
where smells can't
but you still search seeing smells on sites as your own
bitterness

the more of you creaturely insistence

the more the internet seems made
in meaningless without conquence
you revel
smelling
onions
which smell like onions

you sit naked, hot underneath your clothes
in leather,
your star sign stupid glowing the dark,
your avatar aflamed
your back clean
typing writing with a nameless scent of technology

you think
o still the smell of amazon prime

you love paying hundreds of pounds for things you hate

paint on your open back
a big red circle still

and in the circle you let people write on you

write on the middle of your back what your smell is

so people can see
and with this information, you can write your story
in ten lines or one thousand pages

and with this written
you never wash again

pits

There are people so cleanly scrubbed / that when they
pass / even a dog wouldn't growl / though they are
neither holy / nor humble.

Stanislaw Grochowiak

oall your future
like a pit

and you do the classic lean
your head across down on your own
tit and take a smell
of your own pit
and you think of rhyme and hair
what lingers like blood on the tip
of a needle and you think wow
this is completely acceptable
until someone else is
and then it depends on
your relationship with them

full of noodles
you judge the living
with your smell

through two of five gaps in your face
you have no brain
to speak of

only the nose
less
one waiting

you are free

and appetising
a return to the devil's glass
that is dualing pure

waiting
stayed off by spraying all
foreign and rotten

stabvest for the headless you
think

spraying
you smell love, in the fox
bins food on the road

you drink other people's tea
because it smells different
half drunk

I mean, you go to tables in cafes
and eat leftover food

half eaten
you imagine their saliva in the croissant
and sniff the bite marks

you wait and squeeze the white spot lump

your micro pit

in your neck

and smell what comes out and it smells

of not your neck

which organs do you think smell the worst?

in or out of the body?

a change of perspective could do no harm

and a shave

does olfactory acuity increase with the removal of another

sense?

you try to cook with a blindfold, but you use a microwave

so all you smell is the plastic buckling

and a miniature nuclear reactor going off on one

and the melting

and you remember the smell of ants burning

and you take off the mask

liver fresh from the butchers

rreeks

straight in the bin

a finger twirling around hair, but where on the body?

if hairs grow in they hurt you bad
if they are out and on a body you don't
and find attractive
they carry smells from the body that twitch trip
the mind into your wish

rain smells of nothing
and people who say it does have no thoughts of water
why do we let hair grow?

seafood and chicken opened after a few days in its mandarin
juices

you're letting it rot to cover yours

give it a wash, smell your fingers again

don't flush

volunteer for medical experiments

you are out of bacterial washes

it's all coming to get you
she or he looks at you funny as you inhale

you can't waste what you like

waste you pine it

waste employee won't travel by plane, only by train,
because of the environment they get fired waste

you don't mind if it's yours, or his or hers,
but if it's anyone else's,
it is disgusting in a warning way

waste you examine that which is on your fingers

him or her slips the black dot on your inside leg
from out of your skin
and retches unexpectedly and stays around
before washing their hands, quietly and reasonably

waste the theme of ineffectual armour comes

not a lot of people writing much think about stab vests
of the actual kind, but everything they is about the other kind
invisible unreal

like the smell of brains

the brains through the nose
clever clogs

betrayed by the space between arm and chest

double nature was never so stupid
as to when
two eyes, two lips, two feet
both right and left
became two nostrils

congenial

asserting the hell is not of making

but smelling
the smell of absence

kidding no one, lieing with de-odorant

the think of all you want, metal can,
all you can have

just don't let me down, you say
ill pay
don't let me know
put something back into me
please spray don't roll into flame
don't burst into amazing pieces
one will go into me and that which is burst
will leak liquid and that will smell even worse

please animal
do not me with be
in dark moments
when I cannot myself
and wear and how
I will be appearing
to those "communities"

you signed signature to protect please
do not shrapnel me
for you have never used that word before

the hairs fall from your armpit like insect legs

or ordinance
and will never, truly, stop
unless you de-odorise
flammable natures and
pop

and do not kill you but offer you a root to rot
to the worse word
damned infectio major

this your words is an infection words,
but one no doctor can diagnose
and because you rely

your doctor they too, stink

you take a huge breath of air and your lungs are absent

your nose is busy

smell them inflating outside of your body

you think of an eagle and what, underwing, it reeks of

freedom and how you'd not know what to do

with waste it complaining about yourself
and how you can't even use a bidet

after all that
you get home hungry, after all that,
in a haze of a hopeful simple recipe

as comforting to imagine, like tagine,
you can consume the earth with ingredients
that hide you

for a mammoth slab of rock is your kitchen,
and is well good cooking, you learned it

and don't worry about why they are alone
or what others smell
or how one is that way
sensorily

but instead ask
smelling old breast

why won't it cook through the sauce?

why is spice?
you sneeze and worry for a second
thinking you won't smell well again

but cannibal dreams

you watch the terror
mock crawl
across your room
in
pieces of human

you eat skin
from your
neighbour's
dish

you think where is anthrax?
oo almonds

you think lavender, old dog, you squeeze

where is rancid mushrooms, or mossy

where's the cemetery?

hunger has
no
its limits

you smell the food in your fridge you check for expiry
the diary is expired
so is the cathedral city
the pesto has the mold on it
such a different colour but smelling the same
the vegetables are all gone but it is the black banana
you hold to your nose

stay put, you think, I'll be back in a minute
this will mash against my skin I can put it nowhere

the new dignity is to say nothing
as double nature was never so stupid
as to when two eyes two lips two feet both right and left
became two nostrils

be yourself the ad suggests
but what if yourself stinks of fish?

then you inspire others and join the sea where you will actually
be accepted
underwater

it's the smell of xmas already
only it's not

30 Best Smells In the World

Yet, another reason to work out. Scientists say exercise will help you keep your sense of smell. Don't, and you could end up not being able to enjoy these scents...

1. Cookies Fresh Out the Oven
NO EXPLANATION NECESSARY.

2. Melting Chocolate
Because... chocolate.

3. "Boy" Smell
Right out the shower preferred.

4. Coffee Brewing In the Morning
In voice HELLOOOO!

5. Grass Right After It's Mowed
Makes you feel like it's

6. Bacon
First you sniff, then you surrender your taste buds.

7. Vanilla
Pure bliss, right here.

8. New Car Smell
Sweet scent of accomplishment.

9. Fresh Air
Just breatheee.

10. Coconut
Like a brief getaway to a tropical island.

11. Clothes Fresh Out the Drier
This is what being clean smells like.

12. Pizza
All your hunger pains can be cured with this scent.

13. Oranges
Mmm, vitamin c.

14. Seawater
Life can be a beach.

15. Burning Wood
Makes you think of camp and that time you... nvm.

16. Morning Dew in the Countryside
This is called clean air.

17. Home Smell
Nothing like home sweet home.

18. Baby
Freshly washed or freshly changed preferred.

19. Onions Baking in the Oven With a Roast Beef
ADVERTISEMENT – CONTINUE READING BELOW Some
complicated shit your mum would make.

20. Books
New books, old books, library books...

where is ?
you set fire to your sheets and toilet

you watch tv on school holidays

the changing flavours of smells

why when you release into your own hand
does everything
for different diseases
you can guess?

you are doing so well

major MHC genes and pheremone research
but you avoid
because if they like you they like you

you are a good people
whatever you do, you don't come into your room
undressed, posting
doing a handstand
to defy god

you are doing so well

baked beans you finally got to eat
and drop them on your chest by leaning

that's not what you meant but fine yea
inspiratisation forlorn hope
in the way the smell of your crevices spreads
to the open surfaces

green bread dust
just so the smell at your own body
and that it is against the fears of your parents

against the irony being the less they the more you
who cares if you stink?
no one that matters

feet

And not only the mouths are singing, but the hands, but
the feet, but the buttocks and the genitals, and the whole
creature liquefying into sound, voice and rhythm.
Aime Cesaire

you feet were breathing and you
said go
leave me toes

so dark so you
You who has to wait for help to move
a power moves you
to put you in place

trust nothing that doesn't smell

the lowest form of human knowledge
is describing smells in words

yet you are listening
deciding to add something to a product
you were books that no one will read,
hallowed
you were time hanging

you that which is on your sole
that happens to be what
comes from
beneath your nails

toenails over pits

but then about breathing.
if only you could make some
connection between the smell of your mouth
and tongue and the inside of
your skull as
your insoles have more wisdom
and to them come the flies
and you pay them.
always open, always surprises
a window becomes the view
you see the Aegean
unwashed, you stumble in your dressing gown
to the water's edge
you try to catch fish with your feet
like a monkey
people laugh at you
they squeeze
until your eyes come out your intestines become lovely

like nests emerging from beautiful

achilles

outside your heels

gorgeous like goosey

you bound, arrowed, webbed

saint of the rejecta

mata

effluvia

you walk dead and smells equal

up

your feet are wet

rotting in war boots

smells going longer than your life

what is the smell of sad

mass

in their heaven?

death birth and sex

does right enough

the logical conclusion

the autobiography of Death
for which you have 15 questions

15 qs on the smell of it
coming back, out of a cave

the smell of sharing?

nor standing

smells as images in nature
as the grind

the process of grinding experience with your face
forced walking
without touch
morning awful grind stretch of smells

The feet (pied)
The genitals (unfortunate, necessary, once)
The bush

You
don't
choose

how you
smell. Should
you wish to notice?

the elderly on transport smells of your bin
the young woman on the tube smells of chemcial
eternal
unodorable
all everyone else are fish

fish with feet
unto death
then the juice of disintegration
walking out of the primordial waterworld

it is pleasant to smell others smells in order to mask your own

why won't it do that anymore?

one does not want a thing
because it is good, you think
but finds it good because one wants it

very clever
you smell giving what you don't
have easily
pessimisim as humanity

not expecting too much
you clap clap slit
scratch your bot

you leaf you

you jesus wash

you walker walking

you the single one true
person
the ollonaus
of the morning train
the one who sinks
in hair or forgetful happiness
or bad person hygiene
and stinks
so brightly

the model (who wants to be a person
not another model)
stops their scat
with a corn
and then on their feet
holds to their face
exuding
and scrubbing furiously
on the picture

for no photograph can have
morning breath

mores the pity
no one wants
motionless
charm where age cant come
more than
smelling

the person who wants, eats
and is telling others how
telling you

the smells of anti matter

less then nothing and wireless
not without smell
but with ambition
to be loved by another who also stinks

who destroyed all noses
for you

as death does
on every skeleton

Pre-life
Life
Post-life

using toxic waste without irony
on invisible illuminates
your key is to make people
think they choose what you need

but you are a smell

loud when sick and when you smelled that
smell
when it hit you
you say I could finally see what
my destiny looked like and why you insist on leaving this to
the end

you'll never know
you'll never walk off
or appreciate the fortune of being able to smell like cheddar
or edam, or gorgon zola
or rind even, or whey
or foot curd
the ripe human cheese of the endless steppe

the body produces so many white liquids
for the nose to know
flee, fled, or words beginning with f

at last

one day you seriously plan
to walk someone
in their house

there the smell creeps
like you getting used
to things not happening
as you imagined

you remove your socks and rub toes
and then make dinner

you can go further
you are more or less
you are kept on your feet
you are cold in here
you can still smell then

the burden shifts from dreams

films
and strange line drawings
which end up words

you are the dog owner happier
for the grooming shop
who keeps in how a dog stinks
only of themselves until humans

it is catastrophic to see you how is your new meds?
you working today?
how is bananas?

the heat of the transport puts you out so you just walk
you are on your way to pay
you wish without friends you still have
post the packages that make the money

your love is seasonal
and sunshine sures up the wet gaps
in your bodyfolds
which now are factories
which produce liquids from solids

what summer is the sound of everyone smelling? you ask
the summer in your shoes

"I can't be more comforting than this."

what is the worst smell
you've smelt which hasn't happened yet, you wonder?

the smell of self-awareness
that is knowing you are

and you wonder walking how people
do not know what they smell like?
the secret is,
they do

what is the greatest smell in history?

jesus washing feet
to show he is humble?

you can't just suspect
for you need
imagine

handwashing in the modern age
socks that were white are now blue

toes which were pink or now black

nails that trap pus

and ingrowth as a metaphor

for the love of tourists in on the joke

you bark into dark

a living lesson for a few sense-making freedoms

you massage yourself

commenting the bones

beneath

how many will run up the feet?

too many

on your ugly legbulbs

they are red and swollen

like gammon

but they are yours alone

and to be wrapped in powder

in cases fungus

living off the land

invading your permanent countryside retreat

into minds

your toots deserve a quiet break
so will forever soon get one
gangrene on the screen
and other limb losses that create
at some molecular level
a bi-product
a new lonely piece of feet
you smell the smell of defeat, on legs, and mercy
the smell of food, and bins, for the arms
the smell of bad art, and notes
the smell of mineral water and electricity

you smells beautiful for certain seconds but no one notices

resting is unwise
as being old, older, leaps on you
you're in a forest
and even there the animals retreat

you should not have walked this far

for a family dynasty

you should be nice, and use your gifts for it

you should by your own hands

and you should be a moral moat

full of fresh water

and be where there are others who know more than you like

Tiberius

Caligula

Claudius

Nero

the colossus of everything being tiny

the foot is far less wise than the hands

or ears

and the toes are not so as the hoof

no better than the fin

but always better than the face

for they are at least honest

and take you places

anas

Excreting is the curse that threatens madness because it shows man his abject finitude, his physicalness, the likely unreality of his hopes and dreams. But even more immediately, it represents man's utter bafflement at the sheer non-sense of creation: to fashion the sublime miracle of the human face, the mysterium tremendum of radiant feminine beauty, the veritable goddesses that beautiful women are: to bring this out of nothing, out of the void, and make it shine in noonday; to take such a miracle and put miracles again within it, deep in the mystery of eyes that peer out—the eye that gave even the dry Darwin a chill: to do all this, and to combine it with an anus that shits! It is too much. Nature mocks us, and poets live in torture.

Ernest Becker

finally perv dreams

that's good you're still
in the stage where it is
in dreams AND reality

appearance in a mirror

one day you got it out and waved it about

during some shits you has

you wore a nine-foot tall, hand-made nine-fruit tree
to bear the good fruit
in reference to the fruit of the Holy Spirit

way behind now
you're sweating and the turtle

you say let's maths that x3 x 6 x9
and curl
the burl
and run

and other times you realised why you wasn't popular

and then turned blue
blue brown
blue brown yelluw

the rites of ordure
excreting in boredom
or wanton pleasure
leads you to think of others doing so

you think of the parent of Beatrice
who draws a close stool to the fire
and voids in the presence of their children

you think the old way left hand
now right and shake

strict tenets to defecation
in sacred burial places

nothing is less mysterious
than the solution of a mystery

you think the problem with the illness is that it shouldn't exist
and is by nature not fair
and then think am I ill? or observing

all the same you refuse to acknowledge it is real
because it's *not* fair

if this boy or girl would let you have a jar of it
you might let the Lord smite thee with madness,
and reek, and astonishment of heart
because you smell worse than shit itself

your black water breaking into reality
drips like a tap

you eat in a kind of abstraction, knowing it will
all come out eventually
best to forget the process
best to respect is the thing

the only commodity you can't buy with money nowadays

how authentic is a movement?

a bit of witch meat

a third bite the charm.

really you wouldn't worry if I were you.

dropped-from-a-helicopter
like the scenes
in scarface
is a metaphor
for defecation
the seal tumbles
and hits the
water
like it meant
to hurt it

you start to make sculptures with your own faeces.
because you can't always get your hands
on other peoples

you say 'you're going to regret saying that',
and began to smell the dump in a sink

I mean, you look really sick
you went to that toilet deliberately

you go so often it's a passion project
it just was said
and you just want to say
you were just as much
a part of it
as everyone else

you smell ions in the air

you won't close the toilet seat

you love snoopy for his nose

you got an award (well, a commendation.)

you imagine if they stabbed
and comedian saying falling back to sleep once woken
is same as trying to push shit back into your arsehole

in a way

you think
move. leave. pay. check.

you buy a special key on amazon again

you think it might be because of what you're eating
which comes from you

and is your fault
after all

you've got too obsessed with cycling
and circles
and eternal recurrence

it's like life playdo

you touch your tongue

your head injury has odour
so cheerful

head?

it keeps you sleeping

you take pills called magadan

you sleep on someone else's bed
then your own

you can smell the memory
foam
through the coverlet

you sleeps beaten and insufferable
yet

you
suffer

you sniff their arse and it hasn't wiped
you do worse

does the memory foam remember that?

yes, you make mockery any solo love
cannot touch

yes you accidentally crap in your pants
and think fine
won't be the last time
and keep on in the bus
with wet calves
yes apotheosis of realisation you finally know
why you got so stinky
so you could what others don't want

and the smell of memorial
pervades you

you gett ahead of yourself
to know the old ways
before they come to tell you

you are not an animal
you do not share with the kingdom the dribbling shits
you may not throw your dook at the visitors
you cannot wear your pants two days in a row
you will not leave the bowl unflished
you cannot seek lovers who have no hands

and it's not so bad

its nostalgia smell
you consider your youth
and wonder why

your youth youth
your little times

you consider your future then
and why are you are still one hundred
sweats of beauty in your bed
for your other theirs is so beautiful to smell

solo
mon, Priam, Ovid,

whomever, are they equal to the smell
of the lizard about the clouds

they are no Debbie or Darren or Cathy or Ian

how do the animals sex organs and the smells they make?
you ask, innocently

in the quiet nights you become dearer
to the nostrils buying the phrase

"we weep because the human race is no better than it is."

but at least aromatase inhibition occurs
and you get used to smells after a bit

you stink anyway,
might as well chest
nuts
and feel sick
for consuming
bacteria from a human ice cream machine

it's obvious to you now
verging on really alone that you should imitate
the habits of many quadrupeds
and accept more gently,
and cure,
your crude limbs with aroma
therapy

you go back to a public toilet
for no reason

in a public hospital
and for weight
you are not immediately
discernible in your meaning

you itch and know
and become the continent

you are then reader of the hole
and threatened lack of understanding

you are now justified in the tease
of the tiny white rolls of remnant toilet paper
that litter and live in the cracks of a million
crevices between buttocks
and in so rolling themselves as tiny paper insects
so they are evoking the word cheeks
and it not is being funny
but revelation against the way of the species

being future

to deny they are bloody monkeys

because that smell

from a gorgeous you seek

is as gorgeous rendering

wiped out waves of knowing

fogfire in the supra gut

as is utterly wretched from the strangers

who are willing

or forced

to break the norm

of not grunting as they shit in public

you curse the person in the stall

and transmogrify

you. the one that stinks

the originary

is located behind you

and needs a mirror to be seen

you who runs free of special paper

have loads of books

but they are annoying

close to your bed in humour.

then one about dogs

but you have neither

but then one is a doctor

and you peel a page and wipe with it

like at war

it's disgusting that you've moved it around

and not wiped it off

but how disgusting? not enough not to sniff the air.

for the torn book is nana

in perception of a world in five senses

where whatever is lunch is apostle of the gutter

with impoverished language of odours

and fine nuances of smells

o the smell of necessary anal socialising

how back patting

to be at the very point

what people you don't know call the speartip

how much it is your anual bonus?

to be a human being and being strangled
by such a tight little door
by being alright airtight
apart from the smell
that awful smell
which assaults
it repeats itself
like a cheap regular requirement
or suppository
which is a theme
which is a starmask

you, you smell awful and wonderful
dependent on mood and digestion
like the unspeakables
but this isn't your organs we are on about
this is sade's denial of god through anti-creation t
his is instead the discovering of your own
product

this is your hidden skin

that pours through clothes

on your hair, and neck, and fingernails

again, in particles

of anti-earth

underland desert

the arctic waste of self

and how it drives you forward

to batter everyone to death with it

to bend over and speak

only you stink too much to kill

and you couldn't not a fly

because no one dies

and insects are made of plastic

and there are parasitic maladies in their needle noses

which maybe stabbed in veins on some bonfire

your weapon allured

and you smelled of whatever you liked

down there lemons

anal lavender

and bumhole sandpaper

but not now, because this smell
is not early onset
it's the opposite
like a musk
it does not attract, but expels

like in your memory, but much more
like enough to know you are still
shitting
after all these years

you realise your ideas make you

and sat on the toilet
never squatting
you couldn't inspire
it to speed up
so how in control are you?

you think deep anti verbal desire inside to die is the problem?

not what you're saying

but what you're doing

it's almost as if the smell of the open being
out in it doesn't help that much or that often

you smell a rat
you think if you can't keep your scent to yourself
you might as well keep your feelings where they belong
stuffed up inside yourself like a drug ball
or a constipaty
or a beetle's frame
inside the angioplasty of your being

o you think, what does the inner vein smell of?
you can reach in and find out
but you wont
because they have arrived and they need the bathroom

genitae

We know very well what there is under other people's
tails, but we cannot live without sniffing.

Miroslav Krleza

Quite controllable attraction
around now you aren't very attractive

like an internal editation
of your pervert

furtive but not ashamed fucking pervert

endless perversions committed without lust

all neurotic, and many others too
exception to the fact that
inter urinas et faeces nascimur

whack comes the smell of sexual desire
you've left yourself no space to appreciate

the first sense

of smell

is sexual

again

isn't it?

you want to have sex more than
is possible

but not have sex at all
with thought to fear that comes with folly
fondling

now you, belly is full

the element of what
others
smells
might bring

is putting steps
inside you

inside your or

electricity and online porn
can't make
the smell of shelter

so you find a cave and before going inside
you knock according to the custom
but there is no answer, so you go in
and you see a figure, seated
and you reach out your hand and touch their arm
and it crumbles into dust in your fingers
and you feel their body and realise

but that's not what you are experiencing
so you get up and need only dig a tiny hole
narrow and shallow, to put the dust in
in and out and the figure becomes small and new
and disgusting and you wake up screaming erect or wet
and realise forever

there have been no smells

they were face dreams
and you were just always
having sex alone with yourself
with plugs in your nose
and when they removed nothing
nothing when they're there or not

and so sadly
the next cave
you are on call in a candle shop
and the chemical smell of cinnamon
seems to be bleeding your blood
and you throw up violently
as though a penis was stuffed down your gullet
or the fingers of a corpse
and in the back room cupboard café
there is a cupcake made of organs
and he or she smears it

and you say fine

for you just go with it always

and they do notice how rancid

you smell

but are allowed to

and you think finally

finally

ive found love

and your thick orbs swell

and you wake up fine but do not get out of bed

not feeling like washing

and you laugh

because what else has been going on?

for they are with you

you remember

so you do both of these things well

you just think lie down and let me smell you

in your groin

and all will be well

because I need it to switch

to be back into the prometheon

with the birds and the monkeys and the cats

who will come back

and lube or fill

and my pores will sure

and the smell of the horn

will actually make noise
and urinate even
in the sky

and their feet after a long day of travelling

and the person next to them on that bus or plane
in their t-shirt,
with what is escaping beneath it
that you are not necessarily against until you see their face

their sexual organs then
hidden away
but after sport or exercise
oncoherent
after a pull
or deep lunger

how odd humans lie in wait for animals
coherent
judges
but too vain old or young to not follow
goonish uncertainties of groin

you remember someone

who seemed

deliberately not wash to use their body odour

as a weapon of a kind

and you think now

if only I was that clever

I could've had love long ago

and then that someone becomes this time

and they seem not to notice

and you can only become aroused when they smell

and you tell them not to wash

and if they were real

they wouldn't

the smell of meat

the smell of discharge

the smell of patterns

the smell of hiding

but where does every single creature come from you giant
frame?

why no one concerns

why certain persversions aren't choicey

but wait

but others

are

why some are before

you are the smell
after you've touched it
but not as honest

you drip down into animal economie
to pick up the bird mentioned above
for they have beaks, and no noses

you are the break
beak
the knuckle
funt
the bun
hole

you are the second hole, the third hole
the tasty foal

as an animal might be?

foxes have bone penises
there's an enemy of feeling

that doesn't work hopefully

but you
it comes from
your mind
what is hopeful
is movement
what moves you
is you home between homes
one above shoulders one below

to do this as best as one can
is worth a body

your tears of gold in a potanto
your shape a veg

your smell your fingers
to start the engine ether that sprigs permission
under nails
as everything sometimes is

you read in all books
THERE'S SOMETHING WRONG WITH YOU
and you promise I'll make it fair
laugh
at beauty that starches you can come talk to me
and decide from there

you are getting better

but interrupting smells as the damage is done

with talking

like an act

conversant with recognising

a daft word here

jumping from the bridge

of the nose

down

subtle

fast-moving

twitch-brown

muscle

fibres

front anuses

back stalks

inner foof

and down there

the dark heart-to-heart

which is supposed to be busy, removing nerves from work

healthy unsolaced cited

olfactory

opionion

tuna sandwich as slow mercury

the uncircum

cised

mutilation

song

of heights

of bleach and the public access

to care

when needed

with online spouses

who wed, woo or grumble

and follow your way like little sparkles of lips

that smell like an owl

away, away you are you are with the rubber

around and up you

travelling the treadmill going nowhere

but the smell of rubber

reading the diaries of morbid scripts illegible

what are they talking about?

what was it like before people were aware?

stealing kittens from themselves

fainting at exactly the moment you are with the one you wants

holding what is

between your legs

smelling of shit during it

forever into the past

reeking of dung and stench and multiplying o lord

history gets worse as time passes

gets harder

birth rates decline in a cataclysmic event

old people stop

and the greatest boiled angel is a miracle of the age with its

minky or knob

out of action

you see a critic that won't stop stuffing its face back there

really dumb younger people

the dumbest like

the stomach

that go down

and is attached in front of you

to your own body

your betrayer

you swallow strokes

to digest

that to write is

basically to draw

your own stains

you think, better sniff it now

better get past the rankle

time is made of essence

you become the wallet

or the priap
or the pig in the pocket
the owl hoarder
you become that old banana sat in the ruins

and you smile
and smile
and then wake up
and tell no one
making it real
and think what is that awful need
gnawing at my whatever?
ah its normal
to want to

well I'll tell you
questions remain

the smell of genitals is the smell of the sound of the summer

and the summer is brief

it is how the new seasons will not cease
and how sweat seasons
are the enemy of the eternally clean body

you can never reach
so scrub up and count your pennies

and I will be your friend who asks you
you spend time in cemeteries?
your balls or vaginas
ever seen a grave dug?
and no, you say, your fond long
I don't have the patience to stay and watch mud moved by
teeth

let us be honourable
and honest
nature advises skunks
better than people

like you

you feel let down
as you comprehend nothing
has dated as badly
as the needs of the nose

you draw crude pictures
you smell the end of them
you crayon everywhere

you go out into the street one last time
and try

you buy lemons and people seem to spread as you follow
as you smell their necks
and then run
backwards

you see the signs of guilty conscience then
well, uncongested, deodorised again

you tell yourself that no one remembers
you turn all their grapes sour
you flick out dick out
you voice your fear beneath the door
you don't use toilets for love no more

you do what's natural
and your something something has no telephone
but it rings what it rings

and it says
of all the smells I've smelled

this was definitely one of them

the body is living

you conclude

the air is not to blame
he lists can be endless

the smell of the sounds is the smell of the nails
and the hammer. which you need for the nails

you conclude

you are not born from
you was born from
you are the end of hundreds
from loins that circles close up

you conclude

you all are ultimately edges
of people
hoping they sit not next to us
in case they stink

you conclude

here are many sides to everything
that commit no crime
and you finally know the nose
and better
as the tongue and the genitae
are worse for the people

as both can't be kept
in the mouth

the tongue breaks the bones with human sounds

you conclude

it's that rat again the ad positivity of perversity

as no golden age
appearing covered
in gelatine and wee

you conclude

you are ill in truth

you are embarrassing

you fear you will crawl into a hole
to lay an egg

you fear your eyes
perched upon
the same ruined nose
can smell

SJ Fowler is a writer, poet and performer. His work has explored an expansive idea of poetry and literature - the textual, visual, asemic, concrete, sonic, collaborative, performative, improvised, curatorial - through 50 publications, 400 performances in over 40 countries, 4 large scale event programs, numerous commissions, collaborations and more. His work has been commissioned by The National Gallery, Tate Modern, BBC Radio 3, Somerset House, Tate Britain, London Sinfonietta, Southbank Centre, National Centre for Writing, National Poetry Library, Science Museum and Liverpool Biennial.

As of this book, he has published eleven collections of poetry, seven of visual poetry, six of collaborative poetry, a selected essays and two volumes of selected collaborations, as well as a novella. Including letterpress prints, posters, cassettes and pamphlets, he has worked with over 40 independent UK presses. His writing has explored prescription drugs, films, fight sports, museums, prisons and animals, often taking on satirical, conceptual and experimental forms. These publications were documented in a retrospective at the Small Publisher Fair's 2022 exhibition.

He was part of the first ever Hub residency at Wellcome Collection, and is poet-in-residence at J&L Gibbons architects and formerly at Kensal Green Cemetery. He is associate artist at Rich Mix. He has won awards from Arts Council England, Jerwood Charitable Foundation, Nordic Culture Fund, Arts Council Ireland and multiple other funding bodies. He has been sent to Peru, Bangladesh, Iraq, Argentina, Georgia and other destinations by The British Council and has performed at over 50 international festivals including Hay on Wye, Cervantino in Mexico, Berlin Literature Festival and Hay Xalapa.

His feature-length films have premiered at Whitechapel Gallery and his plays have been produced by Penned in the Margins and Dash Arts. He was shortlisted for the Republic of Consciousness prize, nominated for the White Review prize for Fiction and his short stories appear in anthologies such as 'Liberating the Canon'. His visual art has been exhibited at the V&A, Hardy Tree Gallery, Jerwood Space and Mile End Art Pavilion, with installations at Kielder Forest and Tate St Ives. His librettos have been performed at LSO St Lukes, Wigmore Hall and Guildhall Music School. His articles and work have appeared in Nature, Vice Magazine, Sight and Sound and Jacket2.

He's been translated into 29 languages and produced collaborations with over 200 writers and artists including Iain Sinclair, Eley Williams, Max Porter and Phil Minton. He has worked to develop the fields of performance literature, literary curation, collaborative poetry, asemic writing and neuropoetics in the UK. His sound poetry and concrete poetry have also become known internationally appearing in the Palais de Tokyo 100 years of Sound Poetry retrospective and The New Concrete anthology from the Hayward Gallery. Amidst readings, performance and lectures, he has given over 100 fully improvised, or talk poetry, performances at venues across the world.

Since 2010, he has organised nearly 700 public events and is the founder and curator of Poem Brut and The Enemies Project as well as poetry editor at 3am magazine and former executive editor at The Versopolis Review. He is lecturer in Creative Writing and English Literature at Kingston University, has taught at Tate Modern, Poetry School and Photographer's Gallery and is a Salzburg Global Fellow. He is the director of Writers' Kingston and European Poetry Festival.

www.stevenjfowler.com

Printed in Great Britain
by Amazon

48754499R00057